PIANO • VOCAL • GUITAR

2/10
784
Mor

MORE SONGS OF THE 2000s
THE DECADE SERIES

ISBN 978-1-4234-8507-0

HAL•LEONARD®
CORPORATION
7777 W. BLUEMOUND RD. P.O. BOX 13819 MILWAUKEE, WI 53213

Visit Hal Leonard Online at
www.halleonard.com

CONTENTS

ALL OR NOTHING

Words and Music by WAYNE HECTOR
and STEVE MAC

fall when you reach the bot - tom; it's now or nev - er. Is it

all, or are we ___ just friends? ___ Is this how ___ it

ends, with a sim - ple tel - e - phone call? You leave me here with noth - ing at

all, all.

rit.

APOLOGIZE

Words and Music by
RYAN TEDDER

Moderately slow

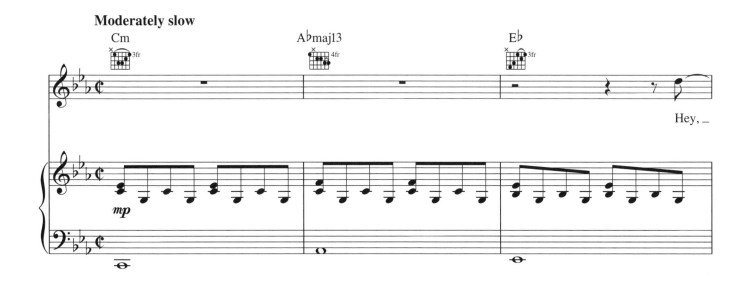

Hey, ___

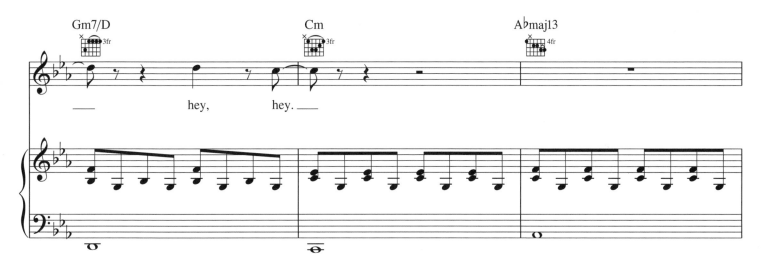

___ hey,   hey. ___

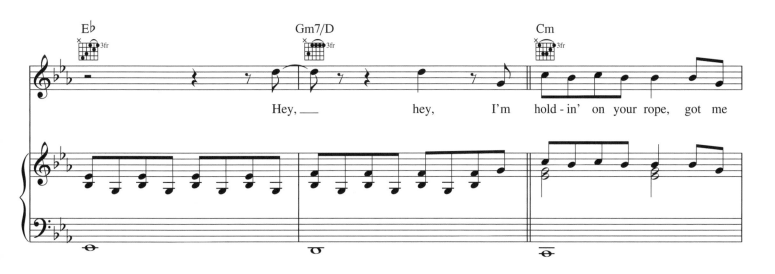

Hey, ___   hey,   I'm hold-in' on your rope, got me

BAD DAY

Words and Music by
DANIEL POWTER

Where is the mo - ment we need - ed the most? __

You kick up the leaves __ and the mag - ic is lost. __

They tell me your blue __ skies fade __ to grey. __ They tell me your pas - sion's gone __ a - way __

BE WITHOUT YOU

Words and Music by MARY J. BLIGE,
JOHNTA AUSTIN, BRYAN MICHAEL COX
and JASON PERRY

BECAUSE OF YOU

Words and Music by KELLY CLARKSON,
DAVID HODGES and BEN MOODY

* Recorded a half step higher.

BENT

Written by
ROB THOMAS

BUBBLY

Words and Music by COLBIE CAILLAT
and JASON REEVES

(Spoken:) Will you count me in?

I've been a-wake __ for a while __ now. You've got me feel-in' like a

child __ now. 'Cause ev-'ry time I see your bub-bly face, __

*Guitarists: Use open D tuning (low to high): D-A-D-F♯-A-D.
    Capo 7th fret (fret numbers next to chord diagrams indicate number of frets above capo).

BIG GIRLS DON'T CRY

Words and Music by STACY FERGUSON
and TOBY GAD

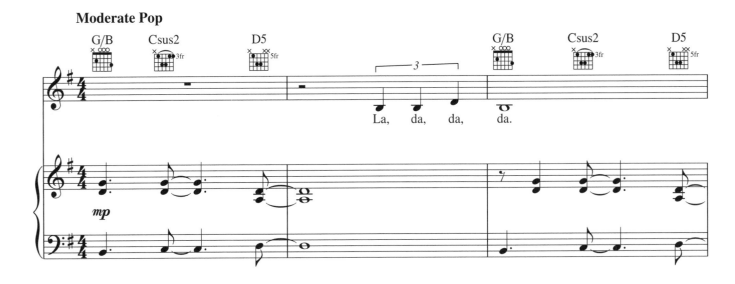

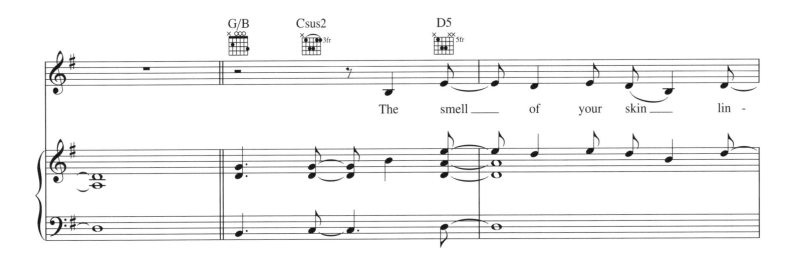

BLACK HORSE AND THE CHERRY TREE

Words and Music by
KATIE TUNSTALL

Moderately, with a beat

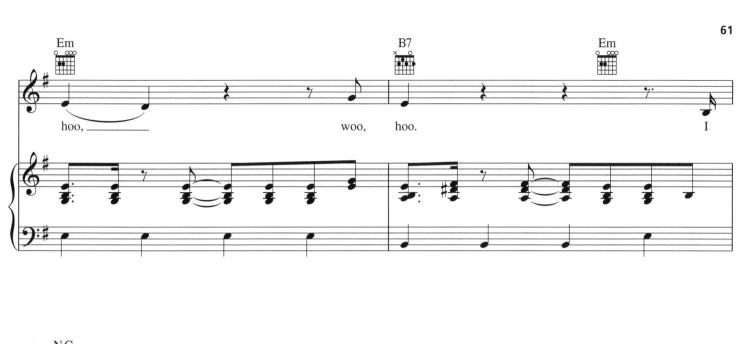

hoo, _____ woo, hoo. I

came a-cross a place in the mid-dle of no - where with a big black horse and a cher - ry tree. Woo,

hoo, _____ woo, hoo. I

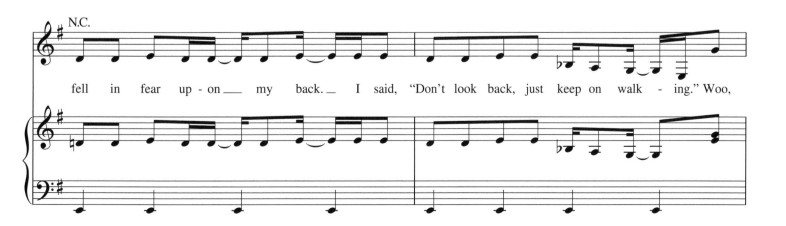

fell in fear up-on ___ my back. ___ I said, "Don't look back, just keep on walk - ing." Woo,

To Coda

BLEEDING LOVE

Words and Music by JESSE McCARTNEY
and RYAN TEDDER

Closed off from __ love, __ I did-n't need the pain. __ Once or twice was e-nough __ and it was all in vain.

BYE BYE BYE

Words and Music by KRISTIAN LUNDIN,
JAKE CARLSSON and ANDREAS CARLSSON

Hey, hey. Bye, bye, bye. __ (Bye,

bye. Bye, bye.)

I'm do-ing this to-night. You're prob-'ly gon-na start a fight. I know this can't be
Just hit me with the truth. Now, girl, you're more than wel-come to. So, give me one good

Recorded a half step higher.

CAN'T GET YOU OUT OF MY HEAD

Words and Music by CATHY DENNIS
and ROB DAVIS

GIRLFRIEND

Words and Music by AVRIL LAVIGNE
and LUKASZ GOTTWALD

Moderately fast Rock

Hey, hey, you, you, I don't like your girl - friend. No way, no way, I
Hey, hey, you, you, I know that you like me. No way, no way, —

think you need a new one. Hey, hey, you, you, I could be your girl - friend.
no, it's not a se - cret. Hey, hey, you, you, I want to be your girl - friend.

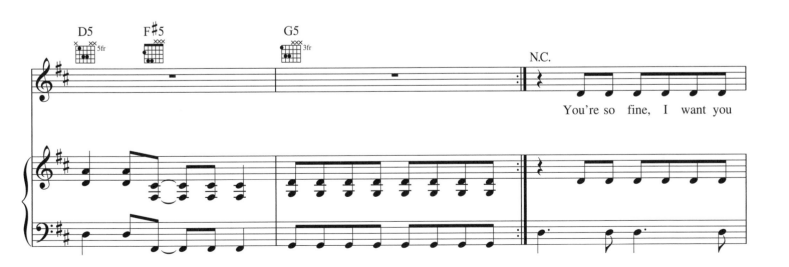

D5   F#5   G5

N.C.

You're so fine, I want you

THE GAME OF LOVE

Words and Music by RICK NOWELS
and GREGG ALEXANDER

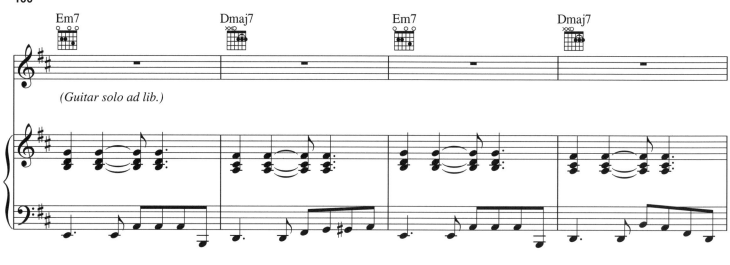

(Guitar solo ad lib.)

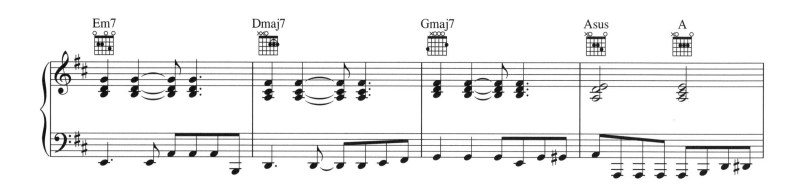

(Make me feel good, yeah.)

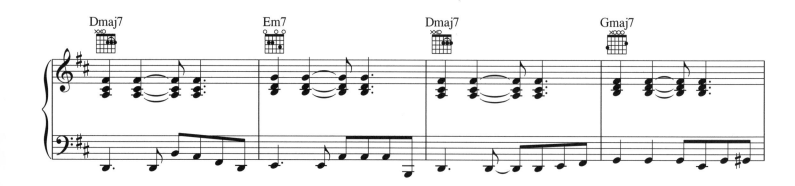

LEAVE
(Get Out)

Words by ALEX CANTRELL and PHILLIP WHITE
Music by CARSTEN SCHACK and KENNETH KARLIN

HERE WITHOUT YOU

Words and Music by MATT ROBERTS, BRAD ARNOLD,
CHRISTOPHER HENDERSON and ROBERT HARRELL

Moderate Rock

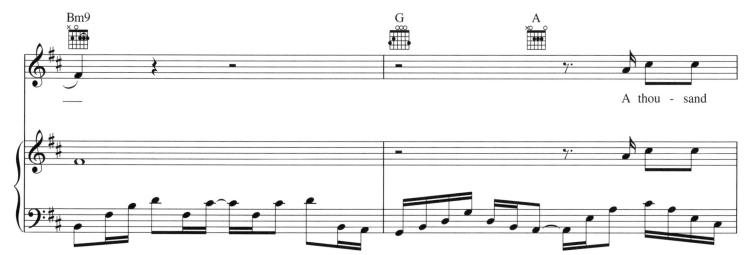

* Recorded a half step lower.

HEY YA!

Words and Music by
ANDRE BENJAMIN

Additional Lyrics

Rap 1: (3000):   Hey, alright now. Alright now, fellas!

   (Fellas):   Yeah!

   (3000):   Now, what's cooler than being cool?

   (Fellas):   Ice Cold!!!!

   (3000):   I can't hear ya. I say what's, what's cooler than being cool?

   (Fellas):   Ice Cold!!!!

   (3000):   Alright, alright, alright, alright, alright, alright, alright, alright.
       OK, now, ladies.

   (Ladies):   Yeah!!!!

   (3000):   Now, we gon' break this thing down in just a few seconds.
       Now, don't have me break this thing down for nothin'.
       Now, I wanna see y'all on y'all baddest behavior.
       Lend me some sugar, I am your neighbor, ahh. Here we go, uhh.

Rap 2:   Now, all Beyoncés and Lucy Lius and Baby Dolls get on the floor.
    You know what to do. You know what to do. You know what to do.

IRREPLACEABLE

Words and Music by SHAFFER SMITH,
BEYONCÉ KNOWLES, TOR HERMANSEN,
MIKKEL ERIKSEN, ESPEN LIND and ARMUND BJORKLUND

To the left, to the left.

To the left, to the left. Mmm.

To the left, to the left. Ev-'ry-thing you own __ in the box to the left.

So go a-head and get gone, and call up __ that __ chick __ and see if she's home.

LIPS OF AN ANGEL

Words and Music by AUSTIN WINKLER,
ROSS HANSON, LLOYD GARVEY, MARK KING,
MICHAEL RODDEN and BRIAN HOWES

Hon - ey, why you call - in' me ____ so ____ late? ____
It's fun - ny that you're call - in' me ____ to - night; ____

It's kind - a hard to talk right ____ now. ____
and, yes, ____ I've ____ dreamt of you, too. ____

Hon - ey, why you cry - in'? Is ev - 'ry - thing O - K? ____
It's just, I know you talk - in' ____ to me will start a fight. ____

LOVE SONG

Words and Music by
SARA BAREILLES

LOVE STORY

Words and Music by
TAYLOR SWIFT

Moderately

We were both young when

I first saw __ you. I close my eyes __ and the flash-back starts. __ I'm stand-in'

MERCY

Words and Music by AIMEE DUFFY
and STEPHEN BOOKER

Hit the beat and take it to the verse, now.

(Yeah, yeah, yeah.)

1. I love you,

(Ooo, ooo,

____ me?   I'm   beg - ging you   for   mer -   cy,_

you got me beg - ging,   you got me beg - ging,   you got me beg - ging...

D.S. al Coda

CODA

G7

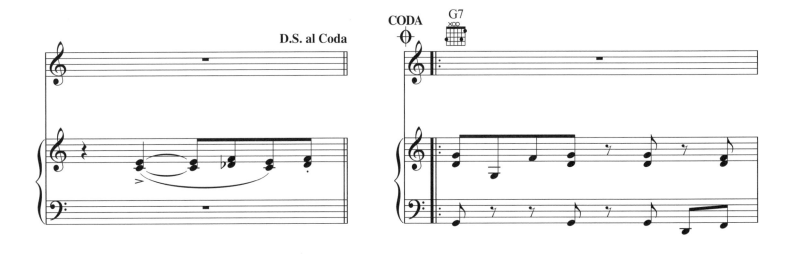

Repeat ad lib. to Fade

Beg-ging you for mer - cy,   you got me beg - ging,   down on my   knees, I said...

NO ONE

Words and Music by ALICIA KEYS,
KERRY BROTHERS, JR. and GEORGE HARRY

You and me to-geth-er _____ through the days and nights. ___

___ I don't wor-ry 'cause ___ ev-'ry-thing's gon-na be al - right. ___

Peo-ple keep ___ talk-in', _____ they can say ___ what they like. ___

But ___ all I know is ev-'ry-thing's gon-na be al - right. _____ And no ___ one, no ___

OVER MY HEAD
(Cable Car)

Words and Music by JOSEPH KING
and ISAAC SLADE

Moderately fast

I nev-er knew, I nev-er knew that ev-'ry-thing was
re-ar-range. I wish you were a stran-ger; I could

fall-ing through, that ev-'ry-one I knew was wait-ing on a cue to turn
dis-en-gage, just say that we a-gree and then nev-er change, soft-en

and run, when all I need-ed was the truth. But that's how it's got-
a bit un-til we all just get a-long. But that's dis-

ROCK YOUR BODY

Words and Music by PHARRELL WILLIAMS,
CHAD HUGO and JUSTIN TIMBERLAKE

REHAB

Words and Music by
AMY WINEHOUSE

Retro Blues

They tried to make me go to re - hab, I ___ said, ___ "No, ___ no, ___ no."

___ Yes, ___ I been ___ black, but when ___ I come ___ back, you won't

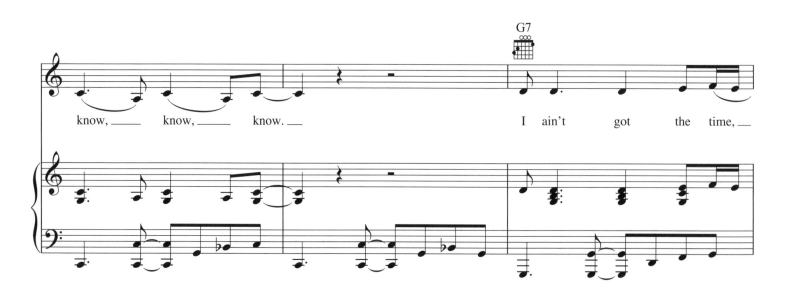

know, ___ know, ___ know. ___ I ain't got the time, ___

and if my dad-dy ___ thinks ___ I'm fine, _____ he's

tried to make me go to re - hab, ___ I ____ won't _____ go, _____ go, _____ go. ___

I'd rath - er be at home _____
The man said, "Why you think _____
I won't ev - er want to ___ drink _____

SAY IT RIGHT

Words and Music by NELLY FURTADO,
TIMOTHY MOSLEY and NATE HILLS

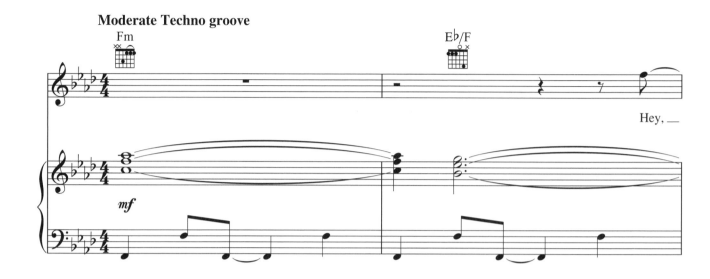

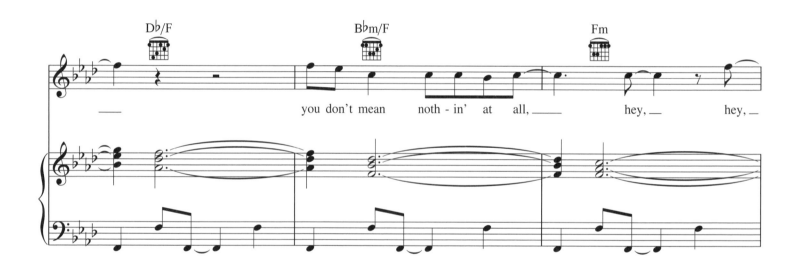

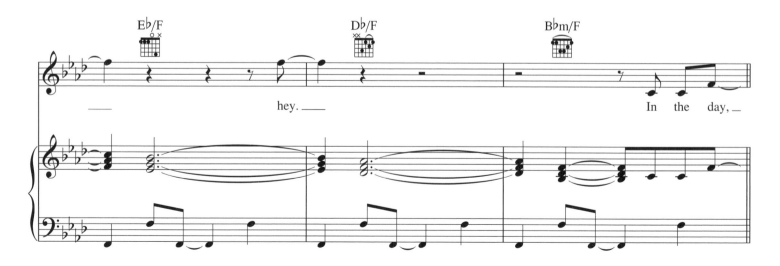

Hey,   hey,   hey,

you don't mean noth-in' at all. ___

Optional Ending

Repeat and Fade

SHE WILL BE LOVED

Words and Music by ADAM LEVINE
and JAMES VALENTINE

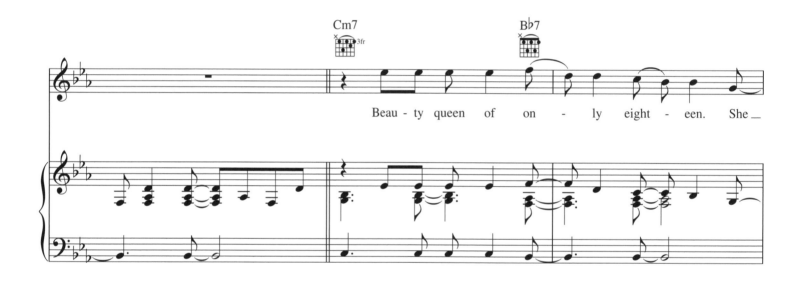

a - lone in your car. _____ Know all of the things _____
that make you who you are. _____ I know that good - bye _____
means noth - ing at all. _____ Comes back and begs me, catch
her ev - 'ry time _____ she _____ falls, _____ yeah. _____

STACY'S MOM

Words and Music by CHRIS COLLINGWOOD
and ADAM SCHLESINGER

THE SWEET ESCAPE

Words and Music by ALIAUNE THIAM,
GWEN STEFANI and GIORGIO TUINFORT

* Recorded a half step lower.

TOXIC

Words and Music by CATHY DENNIS,
CHRISTIAN KARLSSON, PONTUS WINNBERG
and HENRIK JONBACK

This love is dif-fi-cult, but it's ___ real. ___ Don't be a-fraid. We'll

make it out of this mess. It's a love sto - ry. ___ Ba - by, just say ___ yes."

LOVE STORY

Words and Music by
TAYLOR SWIFT

Moderately

We were both young when

I first saw ___ you. I close my eyes ___ and the flash-back starts. ___ I'm stand-in'

THANK YOU

Words and Music by PAUL HERMAN
and DIDO ARMSTRONG

* Recorded a half step lower.
** Vocal written one octave higher than sung.

Push the door; _ I'm home _ at _ last, _ and I'm soak - ing through _ and through. _

UMBRELLA

Words and Music by SHAWN CARTER,
THADDIS L. HARRELL, CHRISTOPHER STEWART
and TERIUS NASH

Moderate Hip-Hop

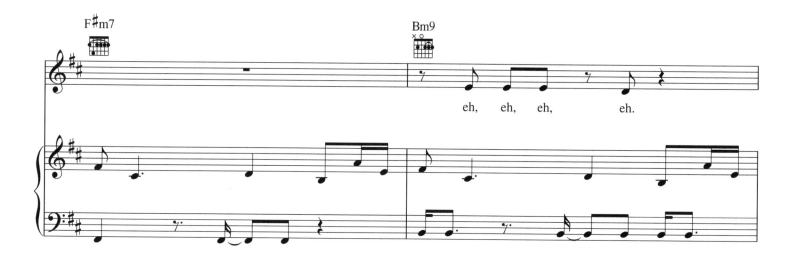

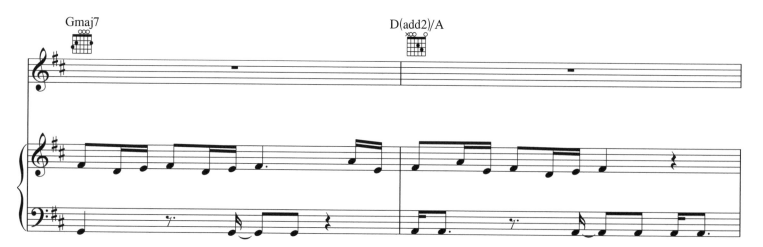

* Recorded a half step lower.

Rap Lyrics

No clouds in my storms. Let it rain. I hydroplane into fame.
Comin' down with the Dow Jones. When the clouds come, we gone.
We Rockafella, she fly higher than weather and she rocks it better.
You know me. An anticipation for precipitation. Stack chips for the rainy day.
Jay, rain man is back wit' little Miss Sunshine. Rihanna, where you at?

UNWRITTEN

Words and Music by NATASHA BEDINGFIELD,
DANIELLE BRISEBOIS and WAYNE RODRIGUES

Medium Pop

I am ___ un-writ-ten, can't read my mind.___
I break ___ tra-di- tion. Some-times my tries ___

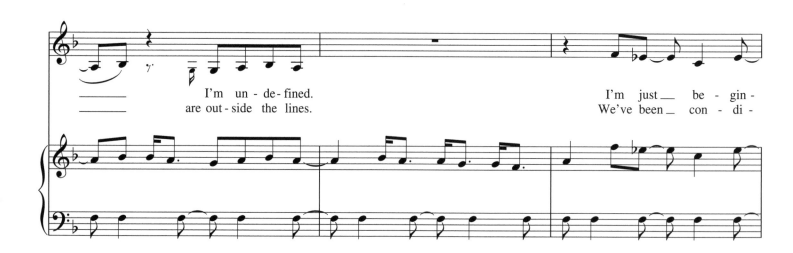

_____ I'm un-de-fined. I'm just ___ be-gin-
_____ are out-side the lines. We've been ___ con-di-

No one else, no one else ___ can speak the words on your ___ lips. Drench your - self ___ in words ___ un - spo - ken. Live your life ___ with arms ___ wide o - pen. To - day is where your book ___ be - gins, the rest is still ___ un - writ - ten.

WHERE IS THE LOVE

Words and Music by WILL ADAMS,
ALLAN PINEDA, JAIME GOMEZ, JUSTIN TIMBERLAKE,
MICHAEL FRATANTUNO, GEORGE PAJON JR.,
PRINTZ BOARD and J. CURTIS

What's wrong with the world, ma-ma? Peo-ple liv-in' like they

*Sung an octave lower.

*Sung an octave lower.

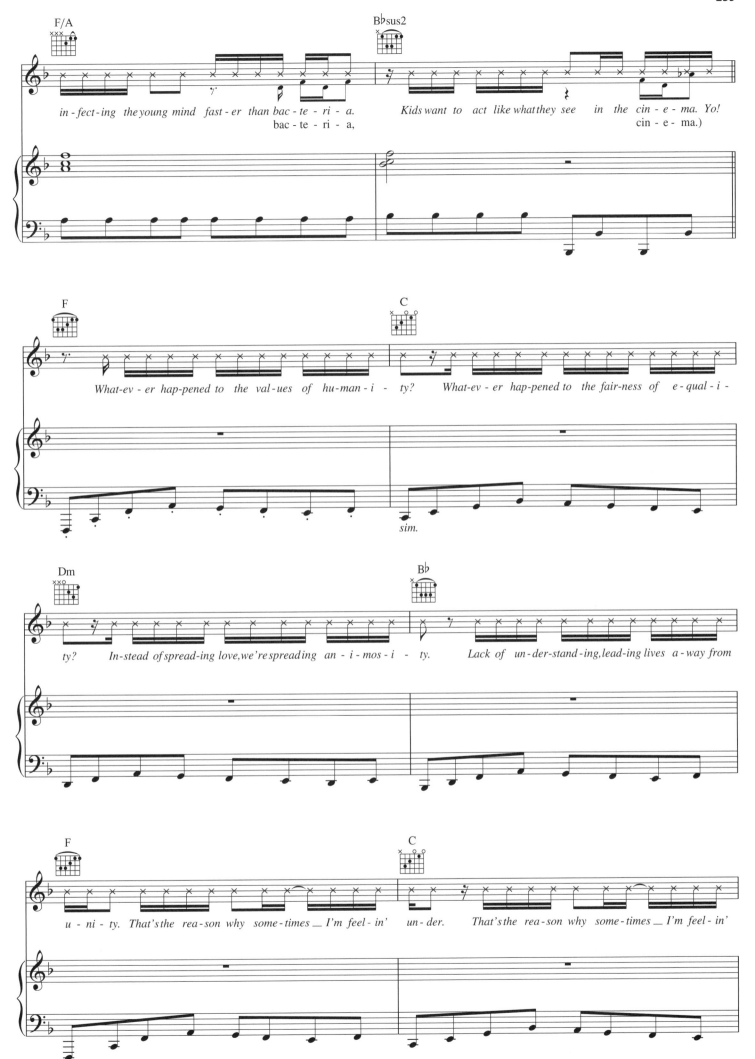

*Sung an octave lower.

*loco

WHO KNEW

Words and Music by ALECIA MOORE,
MAX MARTIN and LUKASZ GOTTWALD

Vocal is written one octave higher than sung.

Bm
F♯m
E
I'll keep you locked in my head until we meet
A
again.
(Until we,
until we meet again.)
Bm
And I won't forget
F♯m
E
you, my friend.
What happened?
If

HAL•LEONARD ESSENTIAL SONGS

THE 1920s

Over 100 songs that shaped the decade: Ain't We Got Fun? • Basin Street Blues • Bye Bye Blackbird • Can't Help Lovin' Dat Man • I Wanna Be Loved by You • Makin' Whoopee • Ol' Man River • Puttin' On the Ritz • Toot, Toot, Tootsie • Yes Sir, That's My Baby • and more.
00311200 ....$24.95

THE 1930s

97 essential songs from the 1930s: April in Paris • Body and Soul • Cheek to Cheek • Falling in Love with Love • Georgia on My Mind • Heart and Soul • I'll Be Seeing You • The Lady Is a Tramp • Mood Indigo • My Funny Valentine • You Are My Sunshine • and more.
00311193 ....$24.95

THE 1940s

An amazing collection of over 100 songs from the '40s: Boogie Woogie Bugle Boy • Don't Get Around Much Anymore • Have I Told You Lately That I Love You • I'll Remember April • Route 66 • Sentimental Journey • Take the "A" Train • You'd Be So Nice to Come Home To • and more.
00311192 ....$24.95

THE 1950s

Over 100 pivotal songs from the 1950s, including: All Shook Up • Bye Bye Love • Chantilly Lace • Fever • Great Balls of Fire • Kansas City • Love and Marriage • Mister Sandman • Rock Around the Clock • Sixteen Tons • Tennessee Waltz • Wonderful! Wonderful! • and more.
00311191 ....$24.95

THE 1960s

104 '60s essentials, including: Baby Love • California Girls • Dancing in the Street • Hey Jude • I Heard It Through the Grapevine • Respect • Stand by Me • Twist and Shout • Will You Love Me Tomorrow • Yesterday • You Keep Me Hangin' On • and more.
00311190 ....$24.95

THE 1970s

Over 80 of the best songs from the '70s: American Pie • Band on the Run • Come Sail Away • Dust in the Wind • I Feel the Earth Move • Let It Be • Morning Has Broken • Smoke on the Water • Take a Chance on Me • The Way We Were • You're So Vain • and more.
00311189 ....$24.95

THE 1980s

Over 70 classics from the age of power pop and hair metal: Against All Odds • Call Me • Ebony and Ivory • The Heat Is On • Jump • Manic Monday • Sister Christian • Time After Time • Up Where We Belong • What's Love Got to Do with It • and more.
00311188 ....$24.95

Complete contents listings are available online at

Prices, contents and availability subject to change without notice.

THE 1990s

68 songs featuring country-crossover, swing revival, the birth of grunge, and more: Change the World • Fields of Gold • Ironic • Livin' La Vida Loca • More Than Words • Smells like Teen Spirit • Walking in Memphis • Zoot Suit Riot • and more.
00311187 ....$24.95

THE 2000s

59 of the best songs that brought in the new millennium: Accidentally in Love • Beautiful • Don't Know Why • Get the Party Started • Hey Ya! • I Hope You Dance • 1985 • This Love • A Thousand Miles • Wherever You Will Go • Who Let the Dogs Out • You Raise Me Up • and more.
00311186 ....$24.95

ACOUSTIC ROCK

Over 70 songs, including: About a Girl • Barely Breathing • Blowin' in the Wind • Fast Car • Landslide • Turn! Turn! Turn! (To Everything There Is a Season) • Walk on the Wild Side • and more.
00311747 ....$24.95

THE BEATLES

Over 90 of the finest from this extraordinary band: All My Loving • Back in the U.S.S.R. • Blackbird • Come Together • Get Back • Help! • Hey Jude • If I Fell • Let It Be • Michelle • Penny Lane • Something • Twist and Shout • Yesterday • more!
00311389 ....$24.95

BROADWAY

Over 90 songs of the stage: Any Dream Will Do • Blue Skies • Cabaret • Don't Cry for Me, Argentina • Edelweiss • Hello, Dolly! • I'll Be Seeing You • Memory • The Music of the Night • Oklahoma • Summer Nights • There's No Business Like Show Business • Tomorrow • more.
00311222 ....$24.95

CHILDREN'S SONGS

Over 110 songs, including: Bob the Builder "Intro Theme Song" • "C" Is for Cookie • Eensy Weensy Spider • I'm Popeye the Sailor Man • The Muppet Show Theme • Old MacDonald • Sesame Street Theme • and more.
00311823 ....$24.99

CHRISTMAS

Over 100 essential holiday favorites: Blue Christmas • The Christmas Song • Deck the Hall • Frosty the Snow Man • Joy to the World • Merry Christmas, Darling • Rudolph the Red-Nosed Reindeer • Silver Bells • and more!
00311241 ....$24.95

COUNTRY

96 essential country standards, including: Achy Breaky Heart • Crazy • The Devil Went down to Georgia • Elvira • Friends in Low Places • God Bless the U.S.A. • Here You Come Again • Lucille • Redneck Woman • Tennessee Waltz • and more.
00311296 ....$24.95

JAZZ STANDARDS

99 jazz classics no music library should be without: Autumn in New York • Body and Soul • Don't Get Around Much Anymore • Easy to Love (You'd Be So Easy to Love) • I've Got You Under My Skin • The Lady Is a Tramp • Mona Lisa • Satin Doll • Stardust • Witchcraft • and more.
00311226 ....$24.95

LOVE SONGS

Over 80 romantic hits: Can You Feel the Love Tonight • Endless Love • From This Moment On • Have I Told You Lately • I Just Called to Say I Love You • Love Will Keep Us Together • My Heart Will Go On • Wonderful Tonight • You Are So Beautiful • more.
00311235 ....$24.95

LOVE STANDARDS

100 romantic standards: Dream a Little Dream of Me • The Glory of Love • I Left My Heart in San Francisco • I've Got My Love to Keep Me Warm • The Look of Love • A Time for Us • You Are the Sunshine of My Life • and more.
00311256 ....$24.95

MOVIE SONGS

94 of the most popular silver screen songs: Alfie • Beauty and the Beast • Chariots of Fire • Footloose • I Will Remember You • Jailhouse Rock • Moon River • People • Somewhere Out There • Summer Nights • Unchained Melody • and more.
00311236 ....$24.95

ROCK

Over 80 essential rock classics: Black Magic Woman • Day Tripper • Free Bird • A Groovy Kind of Love • I Shot the Sheriff • The Joker • My Sharona • Oh, Pretty Woman • Proud Mary • Rocket Man • Roxanne • Takin' Care of Business • A Whiter Shade of Pale • Wild Thing • more!
00311390 ....$24.95

TV SONGS

Over 100 terrific tube tunes, including: The Addams Family Theme • Bonanza • The Brady Bunch • Desperate Housewives Main Title • I Love Lucy • Law and Order • Linus and Lucy • Sesame Street Theme • Theme from the Simpsons • Theme from the X-Files • and more!
00311223 ....$2[?]

WEDDING

83 songs of love and devotion: All I Ask of You • Canon in D • Don't Know Much • Here, There and Everywhere • Love Me Tender • My Heart Will Go On • Somewhere Out There • Wedding March • You Raise Me Up • and more.
00311309 ....$24.95

020[?]

THE DECADE SERIES

The Decade Series explores the music of the 1890s to the 1990s through each era's major events and personalities. Each volume features text and photos and over 40 of the decade's top songs, showing how music has acted as a mirror or a catalyst for current events and trends. All books are arranged for piano, voice and guitar.

Songs of the 1890s
55 songs: Hello! Ma Baby • Maple Leaf Rag • My Wild Irish Rose • The Sidewalks of New York • Stars and Stripes Forever • When You Were Sweet Sixteen • and more.
00311655 ....$12.95

Songs of the 1900s (1900-1909)
57 favorites: By the Light of the Silvery Moon • Give My Regards to Broadway • Glow Worm • Meet Me in St. Louis • Take Me Out to the Ball Game • and more.
00311656 ....$12.95

Songs of the 1910s
57 classics: After You've Gone • Danny Boy • Let Me Call You Sweetheart • My Melancholy Baby • Oh, You Beautiful Doll • When Irish Eyes Are Smiling • and more.
00311657 ....$12.95

Songs of the '20s
59 songs: Ain't Misbehavin' • April Showers • Baby Face • California Here I Come • Five Foot Two, Eyes of Blue • Manhattan • The Varsity Drag • Who's Sorry Now • more.
00361122 ....$15.95

Songs of the '30s
62 standards: All of Me • In the Mood • The Lady Is a Tramp • Love Letters in the Sand • My Funny Valentine • Smoke Gets in Your Eyes • What a Diff'rence a Day Made • more.
00361123 ....$15.95

Songs of the '40s
62 classics: God Bless the Child • How High the Moon • The Last Time I Saw Paris • A Nightingale Sang in Berkeley [S]quare • Swinging On a Star • Tuxedo [Ju]nction • more.
[00]361124 ....$17.95

[So]ngs of the '50s - 2nd Edition
[6]2 songs: Blue Suede Shoes • Blue Velvet • Here's That Rainy Day • Love Me Tender • Misty • Rock Around the Clock • Satin Doll • Tammy • Young at Heart • and more.
00361125 ....$16.95

Songs of the '60s - 2nd Edition
62 tunes: By the Time I Get to Phoenix • California Dreamin' • Can't Help Falling in Love • Happy Together • I Want to Hold Your Hand • Strangers in the Night • and more.
00361126 ....$16.95

Songs of the '70s
More than 45 songs: Feelings • How Deep Is Your Love • Imagine • Let It Be • Me and Bobby McGee • Piano Man • Send in the Clowns • You Don't Bring Me Flowers • more.
00361127 ....$16.95

Songs of the '80s
Over 40 hits: Candle in the Wind • Ebony and Ivory • Every Breath You Take • Flash-dance...What a Feeling • Islands in the Stream • What's Love Got to Do with It • and more.
00490275 ....$16.95

Songs of the '90s
39 great songs: Achy Breaky Heart • Beautiful in My Eyes • Friends in Low Places • Here and Now • Losing My Religion • Save the Best for Last • Tears in Heaven • and more.
00310151 ....$16.95

Songs of the 2000s
35 tunes: Beautiful • Breakaway • Complicated • Don't Know Why • The Space Between • Underneath It All • White Flag • You Raise Me Up • and more.
00311340 ....$16.95

MORE SONGS OF THE DECADE

More Songs of the '20s
Over 50 songs: Ain't We Got Fun? • Fascinating Rhythm • Malagueña • Nobody Knows You When You're Down and Out • Someone to Watch Over Me • and more.
00311647 ....$15.99

More Songs of the '30s - 2nd Edition
Over 50 favorites: All the Things You Are • A Fine Romance • In a Sentimental Mood • Stompin' at the Savoy • Stormy Weather • Thanks for the Memory • and more.
00311648 ....$15.99

More Songs of the '40s
60 songs: Bali Ha'i • Be Careful, It's My Heart • San Antonio Rose • Some Enchanted Evening • Too Darn Hot • and more.
00311649 ....$15.95

More Songs of the '50s - 2nd Edition
Over 50 songs: Charlie Brown • Hey, Good Lookin' • Hound Dog • Mona Lisa • (Let Me Be Your) Teddy Bear • That's Amoré • and more.
00311650 ....$15.95

More Songs of the '60s - 2nd Edition
Over 60 songs: Alfie • Born to Be Wild • Moon River • Raindrops Keep Fallin' On My Head • Sweet Caroline • What the World Needs Now • Wooly Bully • and more.
00311651 ....$15.95

More Songs of the '70s
Over 50 songs: Afternoon Delight • All By Myself • American Pie • Happy Days • She Believes in Me • She's Always a Woman • Wishing You Were Here • and more.
00311652 ....$15.95

More Songs of the '80s
43 songs: Addicted to Love • Footloose • Girls Just Want to Have Fun • The Heat Is On • Karma Chameleon • Take My Breath Away • and more.
00311653 ....$15.95

More Songs of the '90s
Over 30 hits: Blue • Butterfly Kisses • Change the World • Give Me One Reason • I Don't Want to Wait • My Father's Eyes • My Heart Will Go On • more.
00310430 ....$15.95

EVEN MORE SONGS OF THE DECADE

Even More Songs of the '40s
Over 50 classics: Easy Street • It Could Happen to You • Sioux City Sue • Steppin' Out with My Baby • and more.
00311194 ....$14.95

Even More Songs of the '50s - 2nd Edition
Over 60 great songs: Dream Lover • Great Balls of Fire • La Bamba • Love and Marriage • Wake Up Little Susie • more.
00310986 ....$14.95

Even More Songs of the '60s
59 super hits: Daydream Believer • Good Vibrations • My Girl • Respect • Twist and Shout • Yesterday • and more.
00310987 ....$14.95

Even More Songs of the '70s
51 top songs: I Honestly Love You • I'll Be There • Joy to the World • Time in a Bottle • Y.M.C.A. • and more.
00310988 ....$14.95

Even More Songs of the '80s
39 hits: Chariots of Fire • Jack and Diane • Lady in Red • Missing You • Thriller • Walk Like an Egyptian • more.
00311031 ....$14.95

STILL MORE SONGS OF THE DECADE

Still More Songs of the '30s - 2nd Edition
Over 50 songs: April in Paris • Heat Wave • It Don't Mean a Thing (If It Ain't Got That Swing) • and more.
00310027 ....$15.95

Still More Songs of the '40s
Over 50 favorites: Don't Get Around Much Anymore • If I Loved You • Sentimental Journey • and more.
00310028 ....$15.95

Still More Songs of the '50s - 2nd Edition
Over 50 classics: Autumn Leaves • Chantilly Lace • If I Were a Bell • Luck Be a Lady • Venus • and more.
00310029 ....$15.95

Still More Songs of the '60s
Over 50 songs: Duke of Earl • I'm Henry VIII, I Am • Leader of the Pack • What a Wonderful World • and more.
00311680 ....$15.95

Still More Songs of the '70s
54 hits: Cat's in the Cradle • Nadia's Theme • The Way We Were • You've Got a Friend • and more.
00311683 ....$15.95

Still More Songs of the '80s
40 songs: All I Need • Jessie's Girl • Sweet Dreams (Are Made of This) • Up Where We Belong • and more.
00310321 ....$15.95

Still More Songs of the '90s
40 hits: Fields of Gold • From a Distance • Jump Jive An' Wail • Kiss Me • Mambo No. 5 • and more.
00310575 ....$15.95

FOR MORE INFORMATION,
SEE YOUR LOCAL MUSIC DEALER,
OR WRITE TO:

HAL•LEONARD®
CORPORATION

7777 W. BLUEMOUND RD. P.O. BOX 13819
MILWAUKEE, WISCONSIN 53213

Prices, contents, and availability
subject to change without notice
Complete contents listings available online at
www.halleonard.com.

1208

THE BEST EVER COLLECTION

ARRANGED FOR PIANO, VOICE AND GUITAR

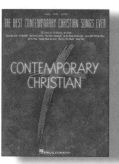

150 of the Most Beautiful Songs Ever
150 ballads
00360735 ....$24.95

150 More of the Most Beautiful Songs Ever
150 songs
00311318 ....$24.95

Best Acoustic Rock Songs Ever
65 acoustic hits
00310984 ....$19.95

Best Big Band Songs Ever
68 big band hits
00359129 ....$16.95

Best Broadway Songs Ever
83 songs
00309155 ....$24.95

More of the Best Broadway Songs Ever
82 songs
00311501 ....$22.95

Best Children's Songs Ever
102 tunes
00310360 (Easy Piano) $19.95

Best Christmas Songs Ever
69 holiday favorites
00359130 ....$19.95

Best Classic Rock Songs Ever
64 hits
00310800 ....$19.99

Best Classical Music Ever
86 classical favorites
00310674 (Piano Solo) $19.95

Best Contemporary Christian Songs Ever
50 favorites
00310558 ....$19.95

Best Country Songs Ever
78 classic country hits
00359135 ....$19.95

Best Early Rock 'n' Roll Songs Ever
74 songs
00310816 ....$19.95

Best Easy Listening Songs Ever
75 mellow favorites
00359193 ....$19.95

Best Gospel Songs Ever
80 gospel songs
00310503 ....$19.95

Best Hymns Ever
118 hymns
00310774 ....$18.95

Best Jazz Standards Ever
77 jazz hits
00311641 ....$19.95

More of the Best Jazz Standards Ever
74 beloved jazz hits
00311023 ....$19.95

Best Latin Songs Ever
67 songs
00310355 ....$19.95

Best Love Songs Ever
65 favorite love songs
00359198 ....$19.95

Best Movie Songs Ever
74 songs
00310063 ....$19.95

Best Praise & Worship Songs Ever
80 all-time favorites
00311057 ....$19.95

More of the Best Praise & Worship Songs Ever
80 songs
00311800 ....$19.99

Best R&B Songs Ever
66 songs
00310184 ....$19.95

Best Rock Songs Ever
63 songs
00490424 ....$18.95

Best Songs Ever
72 must-own classics
00359224 ....$22.95

More of the Best Songs Ever
79 more favorites
00310437 ....$19.95

Best Soul Songs Ever
70 hits
00311427 ....$19.95

Best Standards Ever, Vol. 1 (A-L)
72 beautiful ballads
00359231 ....$17.95

More of the Best Standards Ever, Vol. 1 (A-L)
76 all-time favorites
00310813 ....$17.95

Best Standards Ever, Vol. 2 (M-Z)
72 songs
00359232 ....$17.95

More of the Best Standards Ever, Vol. 2 (M-Z)
75 stunning standards
00310814 ....$17.95

Best Torch Songs Ever
70 sad and sultry favorites
00311027 ....$19.95

Best TV Songs Ever
64 catchy theme songs
00311048 ....$17.5

Best Wedding Songs Ever
70 songs
00311096 ....$19.95

FOR MORE INFORMATION, SEE YOUR LOCAL MUSIC DEALER,
OR WRITE TO:

HAL•LEONARD®
CORPORATION
7777 W. BLUEMOUND RD. P.O. BOX 13819 MILWAUKEE, WI 53213

Visit us on-line for complete songlists at
www.halleonard.com

Prices, contents and availability subject to change without
notice. Not all products available outside the U.S.A.

0309